MIRRORS

OTHER BOSTON CHILDREN'S MUSEUM ACTIVITY BOOKS BY BERNIE ZUBROWSKI:

Balloons: Building and Experimenting with Inflatable Toys

Ball-Point Pens

Blinkers and Buzzers: Building and Experimenting with Electricity and Magnetism

Bubbles

Clocks: Building and Experimenting with Model Timepieces

Messing Around with Drinking Straws

Messing Around with Water Pumps

Milk Carton Blocks

Raceways: Having Fun with Balls and Tacks

Tops: Building and Experimenting with Spinning Toys

Wheels at Work: Building and Experimenting with Models of Machines

MIRRORS

Finding Out About the Properties of Light

BY BERNIE ZUBROWSKI
ILLUSTRATED BY ROY DOTY

A Boston Children's Museum Activity Book
Beech Tree Books / New York

Acknowledgments

Thanks to Maurice Bazin, who checked the accuracy of the scientific content, and extra special thanks to Patti Quinn, who helped me put the final manuscript into clear and coherent form. Also to the fourth and fifth graders of the Farragut and Hennigan Schools of Boston, who helped me try out the projects in this book.

Text copyright © 1992 by Bernie Zubrowski and the Children's Museum, Boston
Illustrations copyright © 1992 by Roy Doty
Photographs on pages 12, 44, 70, and 92 copyright © 1992 by Bernie Zubrowski
Inquiries should be addressed to
William Morrow and Company, Inc., 1350 Avenue of the Americas,
New York, N.Y. 10019.

Printed in the United States of America.
2 3 4 5 6 7 8 9 10
First Beech Tree Edition, 1992

Library of Congress Cataloging-in-Publication Data
Zubrowski, Bernie.
Mirrors : finding out about the properties of light / by Bernie
Zubrowski ; illustrated by Roy Doty.
p. cm.
Summary: Suggested activities explore how mirrors work and how
they demonstrate the properties of light.
ISBN 0-688-10591-2
1. Mirrors—Experiments—Juvenile literature. [1. Mirrors—
Experiments. 2. Light—Experiments. 3. Experiments.] I. Doty,
Roy, 1922- ill. II. Title.
QC385.5.Z83 1992
535'.078—dc20 91-29142 CIP AC

CONTENTS _____

INTRODUCTION _____

The first mirror was probably a pool of water. A Greek myth tells the story of a handsome young man named Narcissus, who grew so fond of his own reflection that he fell into the water and drowned.

When you want to look at yourself in a mirror, you probably head for the nearest bathroom. Maybe you carry a pocket-sized mirror around with you or have a mirror hanging in your bedroom or on the door of your locker at school. Although these are among the more familiar kinds of mirrors, other shiny surfaces can produce the same effects as these mirrors.

When you walk down the street, do you ever stop to check out your reflection in the large windows of stores or office buildings? Depending on the way light strikes the glass, you can often see a clear reflection in these windows, even if the glass is tinted.

If you look down at the sidewalk, you may also see light reflecting off these windows onto the pavement. These patches of light form many interesting and beautiful shapes.

Mirrorlike surfaces can be found in the country as well as in the city. Just as a puddle of water in the city may reflect a skyscraper, lakes and ponds in the country may reflect the trees and sky. When the wind or a passing boat makes waves on the surface of the water, the reflected images are distorted into patterns that can be both strange and lovely.

As you continue looking around, you will see many examples of both natural and man-made mirrors. In your home, for instance, you will notice that objects ranging from dishes to doorknobs can produce mirrorlike reflections.

No one knows when people first started using shiny materials as mirrors because it happened before writing was invented. However, the oldest mirror was uncovered in Egypt. It is made of selenite, a mineral with a shiny surface, and it dates back to 4500 B.C. Bronze, a metal that is still used to make plaques and statues, may also have been used for mirrors thousands of years ago.

The Romans were the first to produce glass mirrors in large quantities. People from all classes of society probably used them. Glass mirrors are different from metal mirrors. While older mirrors were metal having a very shiny surface,

glass mirrors were and are sheets of glass having a shiny metallic coating.

Once mirrors with a metallic backing could be produced in large quantities, they became quite popular. They began to be used not only for grooming, as the early mirrors were, but also for decoration and amusement. In sixteenth-century France, Catherine de Medici built a large room that had 119 glass mirrors in it. Another very wealthy person constructed a mirrored maze that is still on exhibit in Lucerne, Switzerland. The many reflections in the mirrors are so confusing that you need a map to find your way out of the maze!

Today's artists and builders continue to use mirrors to produce special effects. In a passenger terminal at Boston's Logan Airport, there is a long wall made of many mirrors placed at different angles. As people rush by, they see many images of themselves in lively, moving patterns.

Mirrors also serve practical purposes. They are used in many scientific instruments. Your dentist uses a tiny mirror to check your teeth for cavities. Some cameras contain small mirrors that help the photographer compose a picture before shooting. Giant telescopes such as the one on Mount Palomar in California or the Hubble space telescope have huge mirrors that enable astronomers to observe distant stars. Studying mirrors also helps scientists understand the basic properties of light.

Playing around with mirrors gives you the opportunity to be both an artist and a scientist. You can arrange mirrors in special ways to create effects pleasing to the eye. You can also use them to carry out scientific investigations.

You may be surprised to find that almost all the materials you will need to construct the sculptures and perform the experiments in this book are already around the house. Several mirrors, blocks of wood, and pieces of cardboard, plus a flashlight or two, are the basic equipment required to try the projects in this book.

You can purchase a variety of mirrors in the cosmetics or automobile supplies section of large department stores. Look in the school supplies section for mirrors made to hang in student lockers. A good type to use is made of a piece of very flexible plastic that can be removed from its frame and bent into a variety of shapes.

The activities in this book build upon each other. If you do them in sequence, you will be able to understand what comes next. Keep in mind that some projects require more patience and perseverance than others. What looks like a simple challenge may turn out to require a lot of very careful work. So if you don't achieve the expected result right away, keep working at it. Try different approaches until you get the results you want.

 SAFETY NOTE:
When building the models and doing the experiments in this book, it is safer to work with plastic mirrors. If you do use glass, make sure there are no exposed, sharp edges. Do not use cracked mirrors.

PLANE MIRRORS ————————

The common mirrors you find in a bathroom or the ones you carry in your pocket are pieces of glass with a shiny metal backing. The surfaces are flat.

All mirrors that are flat and shiny are called *plane mirrors.* When they are placed next to each other, many kinds of interesting images occur.

REFLECTIONS IN 2 MIRRORS ————

Look into a mirror at yourself and the room around you. You can see straight ahead or at different angles, but beyond this, you are limited in what you can do with a single mirror. As soon as you add a second mirror, however, you multiply the possibilities for creating and observing curious reflections. You may have noticed one very special effect in a hotel lobby or shopping center where 2 mirrors are located directly across from each other. When you stand between 2 parallel mirrors and look into 1 of them, it appears as if you are standing in a series of rooms that goes on forever.

Many other strange effects can occur when 2 mirrors are placed at various angles and positions in relation to each other. To discover these interesting effects, all you need are some simple materials and a sense of adventure.

Making Mirror Supports
No matter what kind of mirrors you use, it is helpful to back them with blocks of wood. The mirrors will then be able to stand vertically by themselves.

You will need:

> 2 mirrors, approximately 6 inches square
> 2 blocks of wood, approximately 6 inches square, or
> > 2 empty paper half-gallon milk cartons
> double-stick tape or masking tape
> scissors

Step 1. Place a small piece of double-stick tape in each corner of 1 side of a block of wood. Press the back of 1 mirror against the pieces of tape. Repeat this step with the other block and mirror.

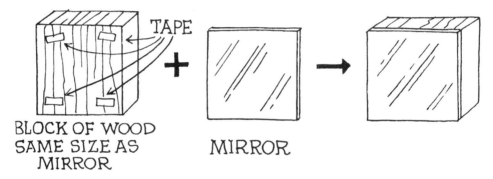

BLOCK OF WOOD
SAME SIZE AS
MIRROR

MIRROR

Step 2. If you are using milk cartons instead of blocks of wood, cut the 2 cartons to the same height as the mirrors. Then follow the instructions in Step 1 above.

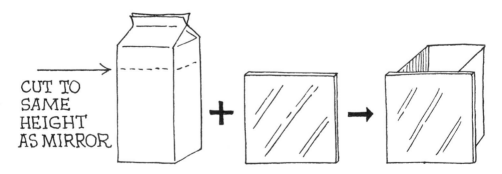

CUT TO
SAME
HEIGHT
AS MIRROR

Setting Up

Place the 2 mirrors on a table or desk in front of you. Rest your chin on the table so that you can look into both mirrors easily.

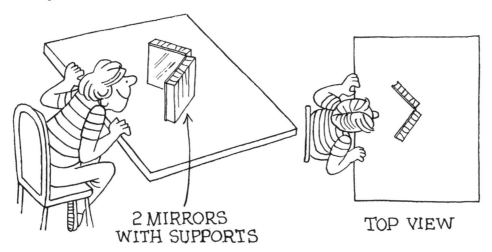

2 MIRRORS WITH SUPPORTS

TOP VIEW

Try looking into the first mirror while moving the second mirror into different positions. Next, move both mirrors and see what kinds of reflections you can create.

Explorations

To meet some of the following challenges, you may need to lift the mirrors off the table and hold them in your hands.

- Can you line up the 2 mirrors so that you can see 2, 4, 6, and 8 images of your face when you look into both mirrors at the same time?
- Can you line up the mirrors so that you can see 3, 5, 7, and 9 images of your face?
- Can you line up the mirrors so that you can see hundreds of reflections?
- Can you line up the mirrors so that you only see half of your face?

- Can you line up the mirrors so that you see most of your face but not your mouth?
- Can you line up the mirrors so that your face appears upside down?

What's Happening?

Almost all of these effects can be produced by standing the mirrors next to each other and then moving their outer edges very slightly. Sometimes only a very small change in distance between the outer edges can result in a large change in what you see.

As you slowly decrease the opening between the mirrors, you can see multiple reflections of your face. When the mirrors are held at certain very exact angles, you will see 2, 4, 6, or 8 reflections of your face.

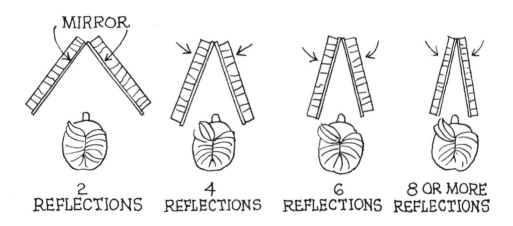

MIRROR

2 REFLECTIONS   4 REFLECTIONS   6 REFLECTIONS   8 OR MORE REFLECTIONS

If the mirrors are small, it may become difficult to place your head between them to see these reflections. Instead, look at the bottom of each mirror. You will see a reflection of the edge of the mirror. Count the number of edges that appear in each mirror. You will see an odd or an even number of reflections in each mirror, but you will always see an even number when you add up the total number of reflections in both mirrors.

If you separate the 2 mirrors entirely and line them up parallel to each other, you can observe a remarkable effect. Place your eye close to the edge of 1 mirror, as shown in the drawing. When you look sideways into the other mirror, you will see multiple reflections that seem to go on forever.

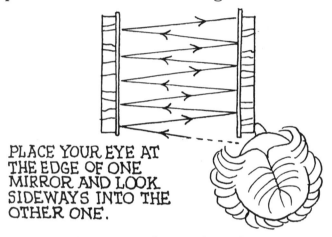

PLACE YOUR EYE AT THE EDGE OF ONE MIRROR AND LOOK SIDEWAYS INTO THE OTHER ONE.

You can also make parts of your face disappear. To do this, hold the mirrors side by side and gradually move the outer edges back instead of forward, as shown in the drawing. You will continue to eliminate your reflected features until you have only ears left. Notice that the slightest move can make a big difference in what you see in the mirrors.

GRADUALLY MOVE THE OUTER EDGES BACK. YOUR IMAGE DISAPPEARS WHEN THE MIRRORS NEAR THIS POSITION.

When you hold 1 mirror on top of the other, you can also produce some weird effects. By moving the mirrors up and down or away from you, you can make a face with no nose or even a face with only a chin and a forehead.

PLACE THE MIRRORS ON TOP OF EACH OTHER AND MOVE THEM AWAY FROM YOU.

To produce an upside-down face, hold the mirrors as shown in the drawing and look into the bottom mirror. As you slowly lower the top mirror toward you, the image of your face will alternate between being upside down and right side up in both mirrors.

LOOK INTO THE BOTTOM MIRROR AND SLOWLY LOWER THE TOP MIRROR.

Thinking about the different ways you moved the mirrors, you can conclude that a very slight change in the position of the mirrors can result in a big change in what you see. This distance and relationship between the 2 mirrors forms a shape called an *angle*.

An angle is the figure formed by 2 straight lines extending from the same point. The amount of turning that is necessary to bring 1 line on top of the other is measured in special mathematical units called *degrees*. A *protractor* is a device used to measure the degrees in an angle. Here are some examples of angles with their measurements.

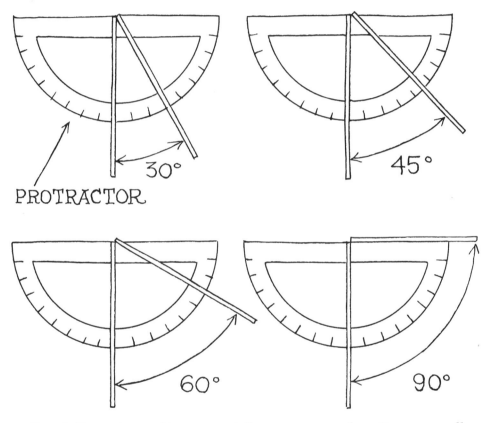

30°

45°

PROTRACTOR

60°

90°

The different results you got from your explorations are all caused by the different angles at which light is reflected from your face onto the mirror and how that light is, in turn, reflected from one mirror to another.

Tracing the path of the light can be quite complicated. To understand more about light and reflections, go on to the explorations that follow.

REFLECTIONS IN 4 MIRRORS _____

You have discovered that a variety of interesting images can be created by placing 1 mirror next to another. What might happen if you added 2 more mirrors to your explorations? Could you produce some of the same effects you created in the previous activities? What new images do you think you could create with 4 mirrors that you couldn't create with 2 mirrors?

You can build on your explorations with 2 mirrors by playing some games with 4.

To make these explorations more fun, have a friend join you.

Try the following hide-and-seek games first; then see what other types of games you and your friend can create using 4 mirrors.

Game 1: Finding the Other Person __

You will need:

> 4 mirrors with supports (See pages 11–12 for assembly instructions.)
> desk or table

Setting Up
Step 1. Find a desk or table large enough so that the 4 mirrors can be moved around without bumping into each other.
Step 2. Line up the mirrors approximately as shown in the drawing. Position yourself and your friend at opposite ends of the table.

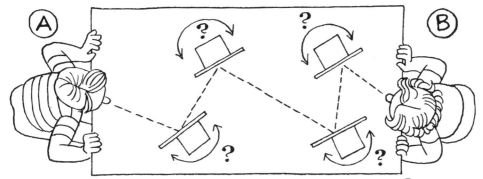

THE MIRRORS ARE ROTATED BY PERSON Ⓐ
UNTIL HE OR SHE SEES PERSON Ⓑ.

Playing the Game

The object of the game is for the "seeker" to line up the 4 mirrors so that he or she can find the "hider" at the other end of the table.

Rule 1. The hider and the seeker must keep their chins somewhere on the edge of the table.

Rule 2. The seeker must move each mirror around until he or she can see the hider in the mirror closest to the seeker.

Rule 3. All 4 mirrors must be used in the search. (To check if this has been done, move each of the mirrors slightly, one at a time, after the hider has been found. If a mirror is really being used, the seeker will lose sight of the hider as the mirror changes position.)

Take turns playing hider and seeker. To vary the game, try placing your heads in different positions on the table. This will force you to realign the mirrors. Try this game several times to see how many ways you and your friend can line up the 4 mirrors and still find each other.

Game 2: Making a Face_____

You will need:

> 4 mirrors with supports (See pages 11–12 for assembly instructions.)
>
> ½-inch round stickers in 4 different colors (Round stickers can be purchased in an office supply store or in the stationery section of most department stores.)

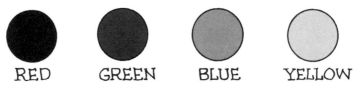

RED   GREEN   BLUE   YELLOW

Setting Up

Step 1. Place the stickers on each of the 4 mirrors as shown in the drawing. Using a different-colored sticker for each body part, make 2 eyes, a nose, 2 ears, and a mouth. *Press the stickers on lightly so that they can be removed easily after the game.*

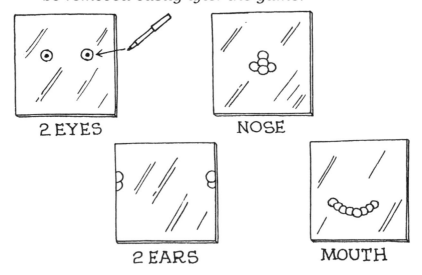

2 EYES   NOSE

2 EARS   MOUTH

Step 2. Stand the 4 mirrors on a table as you did in Game 1. Position each of the mirrors as shown in the illustration.

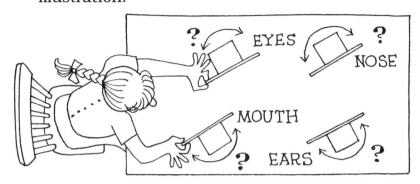

LINE UP THE 4 MIRRORS SO THAT YOU SEE A COMPLETE FACE IN THE NEAREST MIRROR.

Playing the Game

The object of the game is to line up the 4 mirrors so that you see a complete sticker face in the mirror nearest you.

Rule 1. You must keep your chin on the edge of the table at one end.

Rule 2. You must see a complete sticker face in the mirror closest to you. You may change the position of both your head and the mirrors.

Rule 3. The face you create must be similar to a normal face—the eyes, ears, nose, and mouth must be in their usual positions.

See if you or your friend can line up the 4 mirrors in more than one way to make a normal sticker face. Play around and see what kinds of funny faces you can make. Can you make a face that has the nose directly under one of the eyes? Challenge your friend to create different funny faces from the normal ones you made.

Game 3: Lining Up the Stickers _____

Games 1 and 2 did not require a great deal of precision.
Game 3 requires more patience and skill. See how well you
can meet the challenge.

You will need:

> 4 mirrors with supports (See pages 11–12 for as-
> sembly instructions.)
> ½-inch round stickers in 4 different colors (See page
> 20 for suggestions on where to purchase them.)
> ruler

Setting Up

Step 1. Remove the stickers from the mirrors used in
Game 2.

Step 2. Using a ruler, find the center of each mirror. Place a
different-colored sticker in the middle of each mirror.
As in Games 1 and 2, place the 4 mirrors on a table.

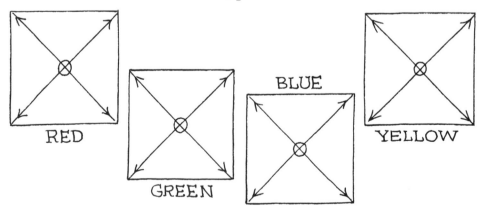

PLACE A DIFFERENT-COLORED STICKER
IN THE MIDDLE OF EACH MIRROR.

Playing the Game

The object of the game is to line up 3 stickers in the 3 mirrors so that it appears that there is only 1 sticker in the fourth mirror, the one nearest you.

Rule 1. You must keep your chin on the edge of the table at one end.

Rule 2. You must see only 1 sticker in the mirror closest to you. You may change the position of both your head and the mirrors until 3 stickers are lined up behind the fourth sticker. (If you move your eyes slightly to the left or right or up and down, you will see the other stickers. Therefore, your alignment must be very precise.)

Once you have mastered this game with one alignment of your eyes and the mirrors, try making a different arrangement. Remember, the stickers must be lined up exactly behind one another.

What's Happening?

You should have noticed that the same general alignment of mirrors can be used in each of the 3 games. One of the simplest arrangements is the following.

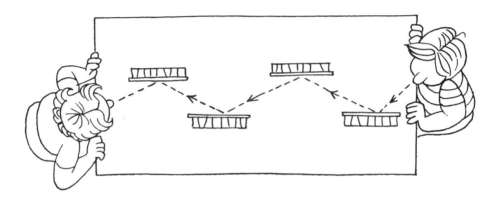

The mirrors are lined up parallel to each other in a zigzag pattern.

Another more complicated arrangement looks like this.

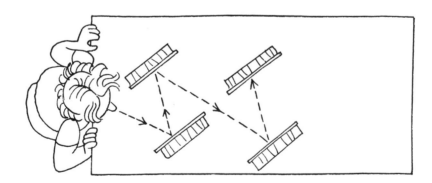

Although both of these arrangements can be used for all 3 games, you had to be more careful and accurate when you were lining up the stickers in Game 3. Did you come up with any other arrangements that worked as well as these 2 did?

What you have observed in all 3 situations, especially the last, is the precision of the path of light. Usually, it seems as if light is all over the place. At times, light may even appear to bend around corners. In reality, however, light travels in a straight line. This is a simple observation, but it has important consequences, as you will discover later. Scientists use the term *light ray* to describe the path of light. Drawings that show how light travels use lines to represent the path.

When you lined up the stickers in Game 3, you limited your vision to a very narrow area of the mirror, which in turn was reflecting only a very small portion of the light. As you lined up each sticker in front of the other, you were mapping the path the light was taking as it was reflected from 1 mirror to another in this narrow area. The light from the sticker farthest from your eye traveled along the path that was marked by the other 3 stickers.

The manner in which light is reflected off each mirror is very exact. You will discover more about this in the next set of games.

HOW LIGHT RAYS TRAVEL —————————

In the previous activities, you had to look directly into a mirror to find or arrange faces and stickers. To do this, you needed lots of light reflecting off the faces and stickers and traveling to and from the mirrors.

Another way of investigating the reflective properties of mirrors is to observe the light from a flashlight.

In a dark room, you can make small spots of light dance around the walls by shining the light from a flashlight onto a small mirror and moving the mirror around with your hand. The path of the light reflecting off the mirror will be very noticeable because the only things you will be able to see are the beam of light from the flashlight and that light beam reflecting off the mirror.

Try adding a second or third mirror. It becomes a real challenge to line up all the mirrors in the right positions to keep reflecting the light. The next games and challenges are designed to help you discover more about how light travels.

Game 1: Mirror Monsters _____

You can just go into a dark room, shine a flashlight on some mirrors, and eventually you will figure out how light rays travel. You can get the same result but have more fun, however, if your friends join you in a mirror-monster game. You can also accumulate lots of observations about how light reflects off mirrors by playing this game. It starts out with simple challenges but can be gradually changed so that much more skill is needed to play it.

You will need:

> 20 pieces of cardboard, 6 inches square
> 20 pieces of cardboard, 2 inches square
> 1 large piece of heavy paper or poster board, approximately 24 inches wide and 30 inches long
> 2 to 4 mirrors with supports (See pages 11–12 for assembly instructions.)
> flashlight
> pencil
> yardstick
> scissors or mat knife

Setting Up

Step 1. With scissors or a mat knife, cut a slot about 1 inch long in 1 side of a 6-inch piece of cardboard. Cut another 1-inch slot in a 2-inch piece of cardboard.

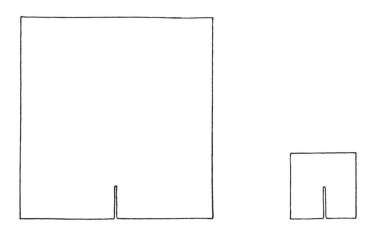

Step 2. Slide the smaller piece of cardboard into the larger one at the slots so that the two bottom edges line up. This assembly should be able to stand by itself.

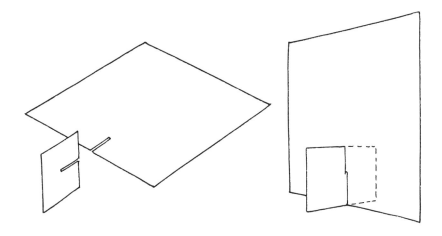

Step 3. Repeat Steps 1 and 2 with all 40 pieces of cardboard. These pieces will form the barriers of the maze.

Step 4. On a large piece of heavy paper or poster board, draw lines to form rectangles 2 inches by 3 inches as shown. This design will be the floor of the maze.

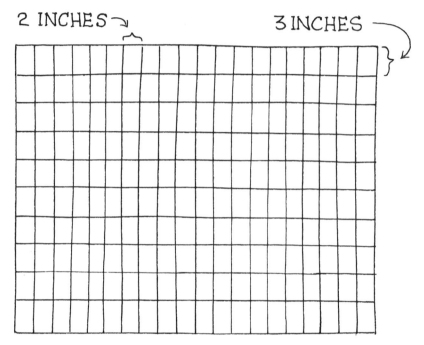

2 INCHES   3 INCHES

Step 5. Draw a picture of your favorite monster on one of the cardboard maze barriers. This becomes the monster barrier.

Playing the Game

The "monster" lives in the secret dungeon of a gloomy old castle where he guards his treasure in total darkness. To prevent anyone from reaching his treasure, the monster builds a maze. But he hates light and will be stunned temporarily if light shines on his face. The object of this game is for the "explorer" to shine a light through the maze, stun the monster, and capture the treasure. You can play this game by yourself, but it will be more fun if you and a friend take turns being the monster and the explorer.

Rule 1. The monster must build a maze. He or she does this by placing the cardboard barriers on the lines of the maze floor. The barriers must be placed on the lines in such a way that there is a space at least 2 inches wide between them. The monster barrier is placed along 1 side of the maze floor.

ONE ARRANGEMENT OF MAZE BARRIERS

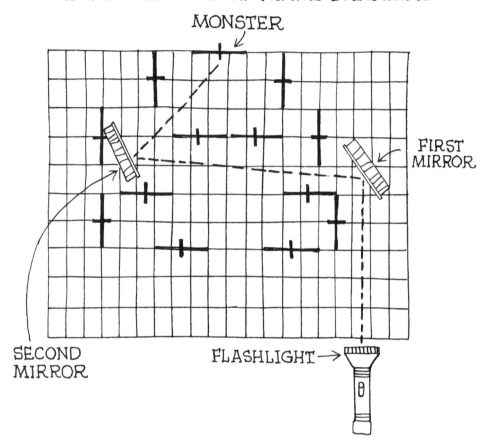

MONSTER

FIRST MIRROR

SECOND MIRROR

FLASHLIGHT →

Rule 2. The explorer must place the flashlight on the floor at either corner of the maze on the side opposite the monster. The flashlight may not be moved.

Rule 3. Using 2 mirrors, the explorer must direct the light beam through the maze in such a way as to shine it on the monster's face. The 2 mirrors may be moved around the maze, but they must stay on the floor and inside of the maze.

Rule 4. The players should decide how many chances or how much time the explorer gets to stun the monster before the two switch roles.

The game should start off simply. For example, the monster should be allowed to use only 5 barriers to make the first maze. As the explorer gets better at reflecting the light beam through the maze, the monster should increase the number of barriers to 10 or even 20.

The explorer's task should also be made more challenging by having him or her use 4 mirrors to direct the beam of light.

What's Happening?

After playing this game for a while, you may have noticed that there is a relationship between the way a light beam strikes a mirror and the way it bounces off. To help you see this relationship more clearly, look at the following illustration. The rays of light are reflecting off the mirrors in 3 different ways. Since the flashlight is shown in the same position in arrangements A, B, and C, only 1 arrangement can be correct. Can you figure out which one?

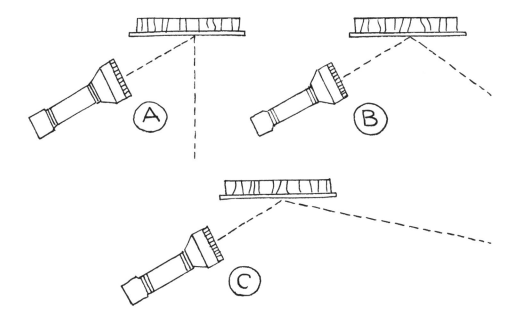

Only arrangement B shows the way light will reflect off a mirror.

As you rotate a mirror counterclockwise, the reflection from a beam of light directed into the mirror will also move counterclockwise, until the face of the mirror is parallel to the beam of light. At that point, the mirror will no longer reflect the light.

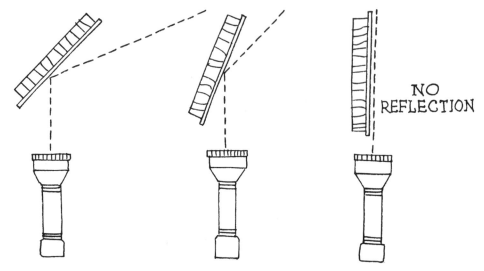

NO
REFLECTION

You may have noticed something else about the light bouncing off the mirrors. As light bounces from one mirror to another, its beam becomes dimmer and dimmer. If a slide projector is available, you can compare it to the flashlight by shining its beam through the maze. The light beam from a projector is so much brighter than the one from a flashlight that you can still end up with a bright spot of light on the monster's face even when you are using 4 mirrors. However, if you increase the number of mirrors, you will discover that even this bright light will eventually become dim.

Mirrors can be used to extend vision and to help locate objects. Automobile mechanics use mirrors to help them see into small spaces while doing engine repairs. Submarines have a device called a *periscope.* This is a long tube with a mirror at each end. These mirrors are arranged so that a person looking through the eyepiece in the submarine can see what's happening above the water line without surfacing.

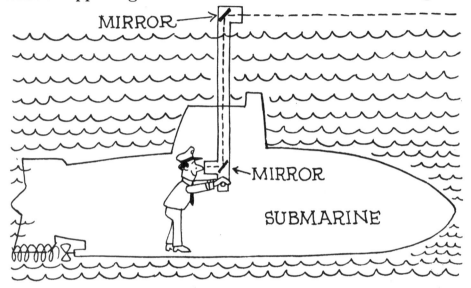

The next two games will show you how to control the path of reflected light more precisely and how to use it to see around barriers.

Game 2: Finding a Person Around a Barrier

You will need:

> 1 piece of cardboard, 14 to 18 inches wide and at least 40 inches long (If you can't find a piece this long, tape 2 or more pieces together.)
> 1 table at least 4 feet long or several desks the same height

2 mirrors with supports (See pages 11–12 for assembly instructions.)
2 pieces of thin string, each 4 feet long
masking tape
flashlight
book

Setting Up

Step 1. Stand the long piece of cardboard on edge along the center of the table. Use masking tape to hold the cardboard upright by forming a "tent" over the middle of the cardboard. Anchor the two ends of the tent to the table with more tape.

TOP VIEW

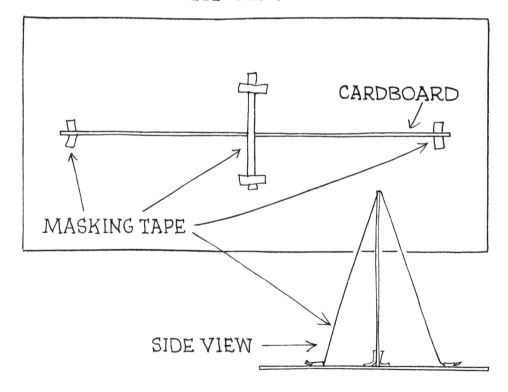

CARDBOARD

MASKING TAPE

SIDE VIEW ⟶

Step 2. Tape one end of one piece of the string to the center of each mirror along its bottom edge. Position each mirror at least 1 inch away from the ends of the cardboard. The placement of the mirrors is very important. To make sure that each mirror is perpendicular (at an angle of 90°) to the cardboard, place a book against the cardboard and align each mirror with it.

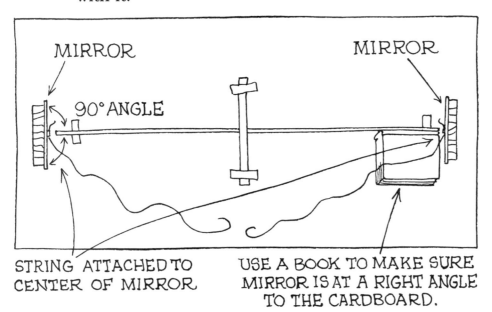

MIRROR

MIRROR

90° ANGLE

STRING ATTACHED TO CENTER OF MIRROR

USE A BOOK TO MAKE SURE MIRROR IS AT A RIGHT ANGLE TO THE CARDBOARD.

Playing the Game

This is a 2-person game. The object of the game is to have the "seeker" locate the exact position of the "hider" by using the mirrors and string.

Rule 1. The hider and the seeker must place their chins on the long sides of the table at opposite ends. Once in position, the hider may not move.

Rule 2. The seeker must remain on the opposite side of the barrier from the hider but, keeping his or her chin on the table, may move from one end of the table to the other in order to look into the mirrors.

Rule 3. When the seeker sees the hider's head in one of the mirrors, the seeker must draw the string from that mirror toward himself or herself and fasten the end to the table at that point.

Rule 4. The seeker must then follow the same procedure with the other mirror. The position of the mirrors may not be changed.

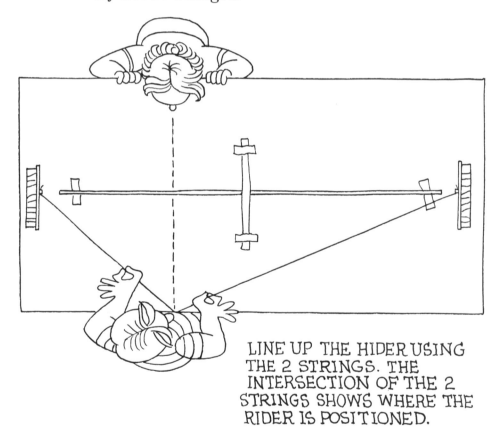

LINE UP THE HIDER USING THE 2 STRINGS. THE INTERSECTION OF THE 2 STRINGS SHOWS WHERE THE RIDER IS POSITIONED.

There is only one position for each mirror from which the seeker will be able to see the other person's head. The string coming from the mirror is used to mark this angle. The intersection of the two strings should indicate where the hider is located on the other side of the barrier. To test this, position a flashlight so that the beam will shine along one of the strings. The light should reflect off the mirror and hit the face of the hider on the other side of the table.

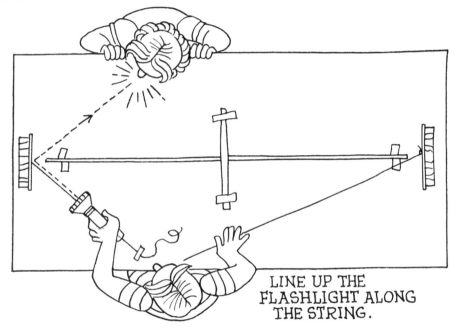

LINE UP THE
FLASHLIGHT ALONG
THE STRING.

If the mirrors are positioned as shown in the drawing and you are careful in aligning them with the cardboard, the strings should intersect on the table.

You can make this game more challenging by setting up an even longer barrier. This will result in more places to hide.

Game 3: Finding the Location of an Object

In Game 2, the hider's chin had to remain on the edge of the table. The seeker's only task was to find how far the hider was from either end of the table. You can make this game more challenging by hiding an object such as a pencil some-where on the table behind the barrier and then trying to find its exact position on the table.

You will need:

> same mirror and barrier assembly as in Game 1
>   (See pages 26–28.)
> pencil
> spool of thread
> flashlight
> ruler or tape measure

Setting Up

Step 1. Place a pencil into a spool of thread so that it can stand vertically.

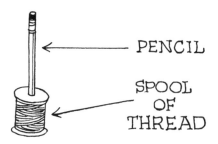

Step 2. Check that the 2 mirrors are still perpendicular to the ends of the cardboard. This is very important.

Playing the Game

The "hider" places the pencil somewhere behind the card-board barrier. The object of the game is for the "seeker" to locate the pencil's distance not only from the ends of the table but from the barrier.

Follow the same procedure as you did in Game 2 except that the seeker does not have to keep his or her chin on the edge of the table. Mark your sight lines with the strings from the mirrors. Fasten the 2 strings at the points where you can see the pencil in the mirrors.

If you have been very precise, the intersection of the 2 strings will show you how far the pencil is from the barrier and the ends of the table. Shine the beam of a flashlight along one of the strings to see if it strikes the pencil.

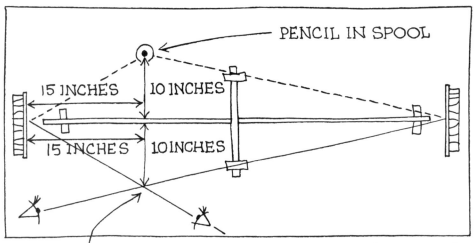

PENCIL IN SPOOL

15 INCHES 10 INCHES

15 INCHES 10 INCHES

THE POINT WHERE THE 2 STRINGS INTERSECT SHOULD BE CLOSE TO THE POSITION OF THE PENCIL ON THE OTHER SIDE OF THE BARRIER. IT SHOULD ALSO BE CLOSE TO THE SAME DISTANCE FROM THE BARRIER AS THE PENCIL.

You can check the accuracy of your string location finder by using a ruler or tape measure. Measure the distance between the pencil and the barrier. Next, measure the distance between the intersection of the strings and the barrier. Do the distances match? Also measure the distances from the edge of the mirrors at each end of the barrier to the pencil, then to the string intersection. The measurements should be very nearly the same.

What's Happening?

After you have played Game 2 for a while, you should discover that there is a pattern to locating the person on the other side of the barrier. The closer the person is to your left, the closer you have to move your head toward the mirror on that side in order to see the hider. The same thing happens if the person is located to your right.

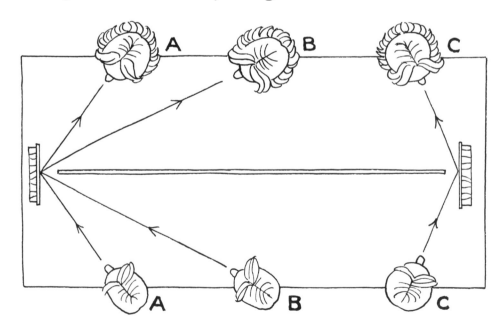

This same alignment holds true when you are locating the pencil. The closer the pencil is to the barrier, the closer you must move your head toward the barrier in order to see the pencil in the mirror.

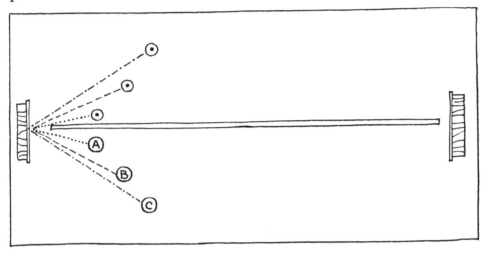

If you think about all that you discovered from the last three games, you will arrive at a rule about how light is reflected from the surface of a mirror: The angle at which you view the reflection of an object in a mirror is the same as the angle at which the object is located from the mirror. Scientists have found that this general rule holds true for light reflecting off any kind of flat surface.

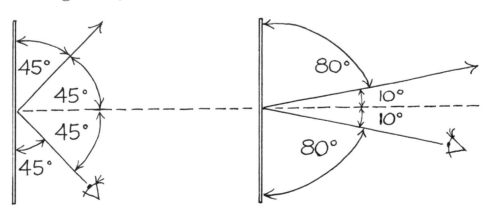

The method of locating objects that you have used in these hide-and-seek games can be very accurate. If the alignment of the strings was slightly off at times, it may have been because 1 or both of the mirrors were not exactly perpendicular to the cardboard barrier. You can see how this happens if you move 1 of the mirrors so that it is no longer perpendicular to the barrier. When you locate the pencil in the mirrors, the point at which the 2 strings intersect will not coincide with the position of the pencil on the other side.

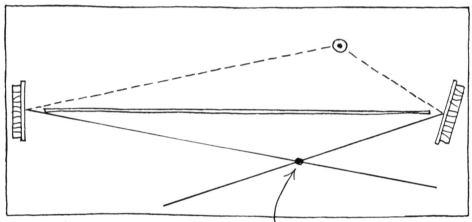

NOW THE INTERSECTION OF THE STRINGS DOES NOT COINCIDE WITH THE POSITION OF THE PENCIL.

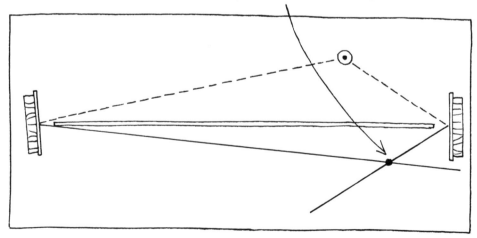

You have demonstrated once again that light travels in straight lines and is reflected off the surface of a mirror in a very precise manner. This property of light has been put to good use by scientists and engineers. Some scientific instruments use light to obtain exact measurements. For example, devices called *lasers* emit very narrow, intense beams of light. Some lasers are used to survey areas of land.

TRANSPARENT MIRRORS

A *transparent mirror* reflects light as well as letting light shine through. A glass window is a good example of such a mirror.

REFLECTIONS IN A TRANSPARENT MIRROR

If you look into the large windows of a store or office building during the day, you will see a reflection of yourself and any other people walking by. If you look into the same windows at night, however, the result will be different. At night you will see what is inside the store much better and there will be almost no reflection on the outside. But if the lights inside have been turned off and a bright light from a passing car strikes you, you will be able to see your reflection once again. Depending on the time of day and how much light is present on either side of the pane of glass, glass windows can act like 2-way mirrors.

Have you ever wondered how this happens? In what ways are windows like mirrors, and in what ways are they different? Can you create the same effects with sheets of plastic as you did with glass or plastic mirrors backed with a metallic coating? The next set of activities will help you answer these questions while observing some curious happenings.

Finding and Using Materials

SAFETY NOTE:
Do *not* use real glass in the following activities. It would be safer for you to use sheets of plastic.

Using some simple materials, you can extend your investigation of how light reflects off different surfaces.

Thin sheets of plastic called Plexiglas can be purchased from most hardware or building supplies stores. Some Plexiglas comes in sheets too large for these experiments. You will have to ask the people in the store to cut it into smaller pieces.

One alternative is heavy acetate sheets that are used for overhead projectors. These sheets can be purchased from art supply stores.

Another alternative is the clear, shiny plastic from containers used to hold salads or pastries. The tops and bottoms of these plastic containers can be cut into flat, rectangular shapes.

No matter what material you use, you will need at least 6 sheets, each approximately 6 inches square. For some activities that you will be doing, it is easier to have 8 or more sheets available.

Multiplying Ghostly Images _____

The entrances to some stores and buildings have sets of glass doors. If you look carefully as you walk through these doors, you can sometimes see several reflections of yourself. They may be faint images appearing in the next door or on the panes of glass that divide the doors. You can also notice this effect at home if you have double windows. These reflections occur only when the light outside and inside is of a certain intensity.

Other strange reflections may appear where sheets of glass meet to form corners. Magicians take advantage of these effects in creating illusions to fool our vision. Some artists have made sculptures which also create unusual and beautiful illusions.

Scientists and engineers have studied reflections to understand how light travels through transparent materials. Investigating transparent mirrors offers many opportunities for you to make new discoveries about the properties of light.

You will need:

>   4 sheets of plastic, each at least 6 inches square
>   4 empty paper half-gallon milk cartons
>   2 flashlights
>   masking tape
>   scissors
>   table
>   slide projector (optional)

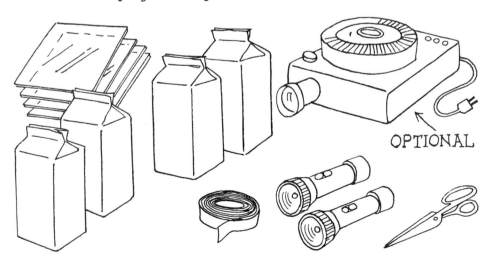

OPTIONAL

Setting Up

Step 1. Cut the milk cartons to the same height as the plastic sheets.

Step 2. Tape one end of each plastic sheet to the edge of a carton as shown in the drawing. The tape should act like a hinge and allow the plastic sheets to rotate easily.

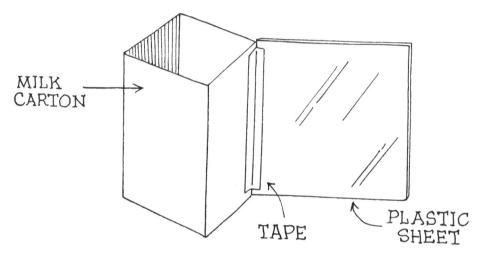

MILK CARTON

TAPE

PLASTIC SHEET

Step 3. Check that each plastic sheet can stand upright with its bottom edge flat against the table.

Explorations

Although you can see images in the plastic sheets in ordinary light, it is better if you work in a darkened room and shine a flashlight onto each side of your face. This will allow you to see a brighter and better image of yourself. Move the 4 plastic sheets around on the table so that they are in different positions in relation to your face and to each other. Then, with your chin resting on the table, see which of the effects produced with plane mirrors you are able to re-create with transparent mirrors.

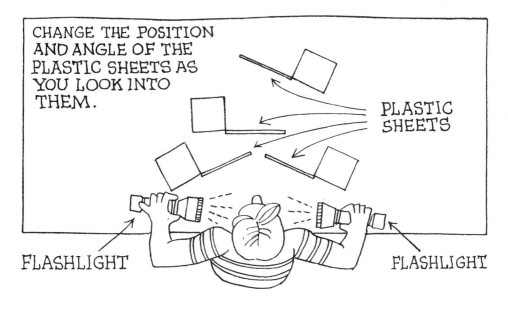

Can you make more than 2 images when you have 2 plastic sheets in front of your face?

Can you make a face with no nose or only one eye?

Line up 2 plastic sheets parallel to each other. Can you see multiple images of the edges of the plastic sheets as you did with the mirrors?

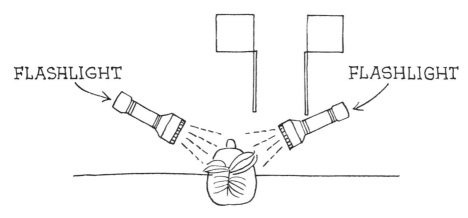

Using 4 plastic sheets, can you make 4 images of your face?

- Can you line up the 4 plastic sheets so that you see only 4 mouths or 4 noses?
- Can you line up the 4 plastic sheets so that you see 4 images of your face, each image decreasing in size?
- If a slide projector is available, try all of the above experiments again. How does the larger amount of light on your face change the images you see?

 SAFETY NOTE:
If you are using a slide projector, don't let the light shine directly in your eyes.

What's Happening?
The results you get with transparent mirrors are similar to those you get with regular mirrors, but there is one important difference. When you hold 2 plastic sheets next to each other at a 90-degree angle, you get 2 or more images. These images are difficult to see, however.

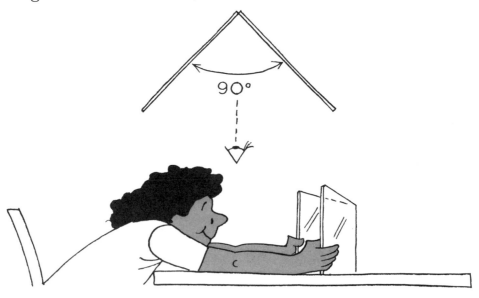

Making the angle smaller makes it even more difficult to see the images. Even the bottom edges of the plastic sheets are not very visible.

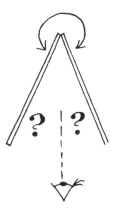

When 2 plastic sheets are parallel to each other, you cannot see any images at all if you are viewing them as shown in the drawing.

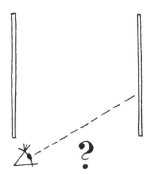

These new experiments can help you better understand what happened in your first explorations of mirrors. When you try to make multiple reflections of your face with transparent mirrors, the images are faint because most of the light travels *through* each plastic sheet instead of being completely reflected from one mirror to another as happened with regular metallic-backed plane mirrors.

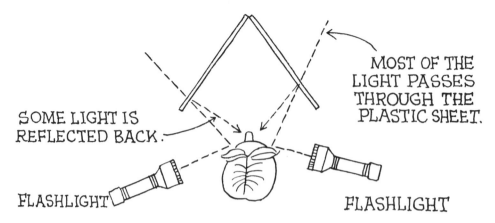

MOST OF THE LIGHT PASSES THROUGH THE PLASTIC SHEET.

SOME LIGHT IS REFLECTED BACK.

FLASHLIGHT

FLASHLIGHT

You can see this difference very readily when you look at 2 parallel plastic sheets. Here almost all of the light has passed through the plastic sheets instead of being reflected back and forth.

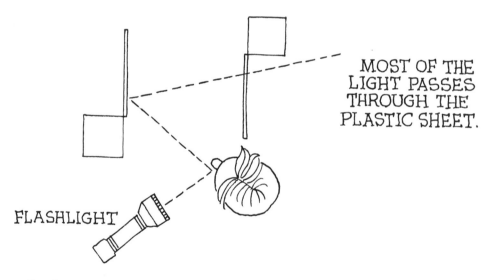

MOST OF THE LIGHT PASSES THROUGH THE PLASTIC SHEET.

FLASHLIGHT

Looking at 2 plastic sheets placed at more than a 180-degree angle produces the same results as regular mirrors placed at that angle. You see a fractured face. Changing the angle slightly lets you create a one-eyed or noseless face. However, once again these images are not as clear as are the ones obtained with regular mirrors.

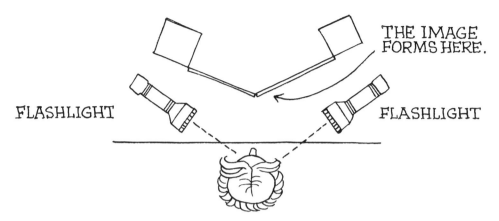

THE IMAGE FORMS HERE.

FLASHLIGHT   FLASHLIGHT

The fact that light is passing through each plastic sheet can be demonstrated by lining up the 4 plastic sheets behind each other. You will see 4 images of your face, one behind the other.

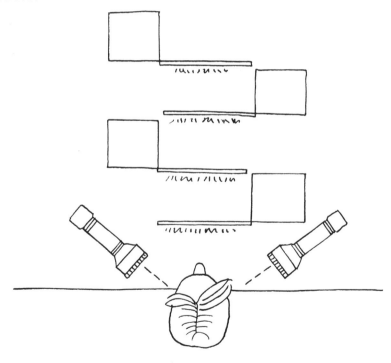

YOU SEE 4 IMAGES,
ONE BEHIND THE OTHER.

As you rotate or slide the plastic sheets, the images will change slightly. If you rotate a plastic sheet to a 45-degree angle in relation to your face, your image will disappear from that sheet.

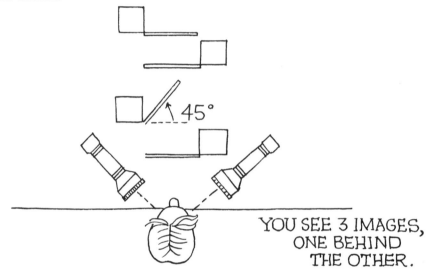

YOU SEE 3 IMAGES,
ONE BEHIND
THE OTHER.

Placing a sheet of paper between the third and fourth plastic sheets will also eliminate one of the images.

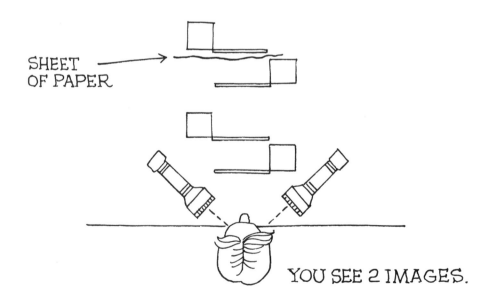

SHEET
OF PAPER

YOU SEE 2 IMAGES.

These experiments show that light reflected from your face passes through each plastic sheet and is reflected back to your face. The more plastic sheets the light travels through, the fainter the last reflected image will be.

This can be demonstrated in another way—by using a light from a slide projector. With this strong light, the images you see on the plastic sheets will be much brighter and clearer, even those farther away from your face. If you line up more than 4 plastic sheets, the difference between the flashlight and the slide projector would be very noticeable as you looked at the image of your face in the seventh and eighth sheets.

You can make an isolated image of your mouth or nose appear in the plastic sheets by holding the flashlight close to your face and shining it on only one feature at a time.

You may have noticed a curious effect when you lined up the 4 plastic sheets behind each other. The plastic sheets farther away from your face gave back reflections smaller than the ones closer to you. (You will examine this effect more closely in the section that explores the location of the reflected image on pages 63–68.)

Magicians and designers of special effects in amusement parks take advantage of the illusions created by transparent mirrors. So do stage managers. For example, the image of a ghost can be made to appear on a stage by using a large mirror and a pane of glass.

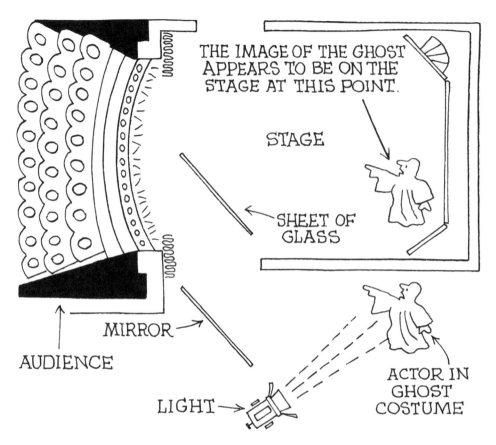

THE IMAGE OF THE GHOST
APPEARS TO BE ON THE
STAGE AT THIS POINT.

STAGE

SHEET OF
GLASS

MIRROR

AUDIENCE

LIGHT

ACTOR IN
GHOST
COSTUME

THE IMAGE OF THE GHOST APPEARS
BEHIND THE GLASS THE SAME DISTANCE
AS THE REAL IMAGE IS FROM THE MIRROR.

An actor in a ghost costume performs offstage in front of a large mirror. The reflection from this mirror is directed to a large pane of glass onstage. Since the audience is in darkness, they do not see the glass. The ghostly image they see appears behind this glass.

The lighting on the stage and on the actor offstage has to be controlled very carefully to produce the right effect. You will better understand how this trick works when you read the section on the copying device (pages 63–68).

A Multiple-Moving-Faces Sculpture —

In the previous explorations the multiple reflections of your face were all stationary. Imagine what would happen if the plastic sheets could rotate freely. You would have multiple images of your face moving past each other in an eerie manner.

It doesn't take much to create this strange effect. This is a fun project you could use to entertain your friends on Halloween.

You will need:

> 4 plastic sheets, each about 6 inches square
> 4 pieces of ribbon, each about ¼ inch wide and 3 inches long
> 4 pieces of wood, each about ½ inch wide and 12 inches long
> 1 or 2 flashlights
> tape
> 2 chairs or 2 tables the same height
> ruler or yardstick

Setting Up
Step 1. Find the center of one edge of each plastic sheet. Tape a piece of ribbon to each sheet at this point. (If you are using very thin plastic sheets, such as acetate or sections of a salad container, use string instead of ribbon.)

TAPE THE RIBBON AT THE CENTER OF THE SHEET.

Step 2. Tape the free end of each ribbon to the middle of each piece of wood. Leave a space of 1 inch between the edge of the plastic sheet and the wood so that the sheet can rotate.

Step 3. Suspend the 4 pieces of wood with the plastic sheets between 2 tables or chairs the same height. Leave a gap of about 3 or 4 inches between each sheet.

Step 4. Darken the room and squat in front of the row of plastic sheets holding 1 or 2 flashlights.

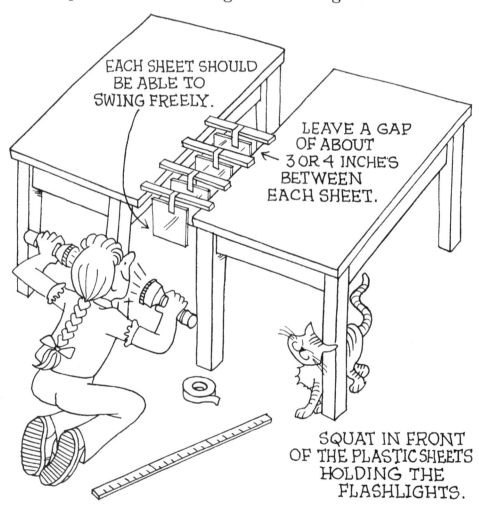

EACH SHEET SHOULD BE ABLE TO SWING FREELY.

LEAVE A GAP OF ABOUT 3 OR 4 INCHES BETWEEN EACH SHEET.

SQUAT IN FRONT OF THE PLASTIC SHEETS HOLDING THE FLASHLIGHTS.

Playing with Your Sculpture

Push each plastic sheet on one side so that the sheets will swing sideways from left to right for a while. Shine a light on your face while looking into the plastic sheets. If you have a second flashlight, shine one on each side of your face. (You can also use the light from a slide projector.) As the plastic sheets swing, the images of your face will move back and forth, producing a very strange effect.

You can also produce a strange effect with your hands. Hold a flashlight in one hand and shine the light directly on the fingers of your other hand in front of the moving plastic sheets. Play around with small objects such as a pencil and see what other kinds of effects you can create with this sculpture.

What's Happening?

The effects you observed are similar to those you obtained from your previous activities with stationary transparent sheets. Light reflected from your face passes through each of the 4 plastic sheets. Some of the light is reflected, giving back an image of your face. The farther the plastic sheet is from your face, the fainter the image. The brighter the light source, the brighter the reflection.

Images disappear and reappear as the plastic sheets swing back and forth because the light is being reflected at different angles. As you have observed so far in your investigations with regular mirrors and transparent sheets, the angle of reflection depends upon the angle at which the light meets the mirror. As the swinging sheet turns away from your face, the angle between the light rays reflecting off your face and the sheet increase. The greater this angle becomes, the more difficult it is to see your reflected image.

A Merging-Faces Sculpture _____

You can construct another sculpture that also creates strange effects with faces. This time you can work with a friend. Your new sculpture will allow you to take on some of the features of your friend's face. As you play with your sculpture, you will add to your knowledge of how light reflects off surfaces.

You will need:

> 8 sheets of plastic, each 6 inches square (The more sheets you use, the more interesting the results will be.)
> 2 flashlights
> 2 pieces of unlined white paper

Explorations

- Place yourself and a friend on opposite sides of a table. Rest your chins on the tabletop and hold a plastic sheet between the 2 faces. It should be a foot or 2 away from each of you. Observe how much you see of yourself and your friend in the plastic sheet.

- Place another plastic sheet against the first one. As you add more and more sheets, continue to observe closely your reflection and the image of your friend. What happens to the two images?

ADD ONE SHEET AT A TIME.

- Find a person with a beard or long hair. See if you can put the beard or long hair on the reflection of your face in the set of plastic sheets.
- Keep adding more sheets. Do you reach a point where you can see only your own reflection and not the face of your friend?
- In a darkened room, repeat the same procedures as before. Have your friend shine a beam of light on his or her face. Does this new situation change how you see your own face or your friend's?
- What happens when both of you shine lights on your faces and add plastic sheets to the set?

- Experiment with the plastic sheets and a flashlight. Set up an arrangement as shown in the drawing.

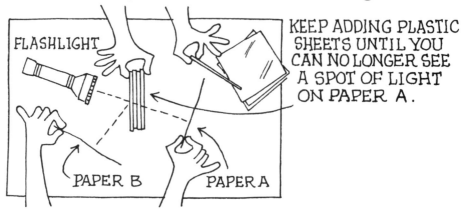

KEEP ADDING PLASTIC SHEETS UNTIL YOU CAN NO LONGER SEE A SPOT OF LIGHT ON PAPER A.

FLASHLIGHT

PAPER B   PAPER A

- Place the flashlight in front of 4 plastic sheets so that you can see the light that passes through the plastic and the light that is reflected back. Have a friend hold 1 piece of paper behind and 1 to the side of the plastic sheets so that you can see better the amount of light.
- What happens as more plastic sheets are added? How does the intensity of the reflected light change? How does the brightness of the light spot behind the plastic sheets change?

What's Happening?

When there is only 1 plastic sheet between you and your friend, you can see each other very clearly, but you can also see faint reflections of yourselves. As more plastic sheets are added, your image becomes stronger to you while your friend's image becomes weaker. At one point, your face and your friend's face appear to merge. Your friend's nose becomes part of your face, while your chin becomes part of his or hers. If more plastic sheets are added, eventually you are not able to see your friend at all. You see only yourself.

Shining a light through the plastic sheets produces a similar effect: As more and more plastic sheets are added, less and less light passes through while there is a noticeable increase in the brightness of the light spot where the reflected light appears on the paper. When you shine a flashlight on your face, your friend sees you better and you see a better reflection of yourself. Add more sheets while shining the flashlight on yourself and you see a better reflection of yourself, but your friend sees less of you.

These situations illustrate a basic property of light. Wherever light encounters a transparent material, some of it passes through and some of it is reflected. Scientists use *reflected light* and *transmitted light* to describe these situations. The more plastic sheets you add, the less light is transmitted through them. Some light is reflected off the surface of each sheet. The gap between two plastic sheets may be *very* small, but it is large enough to allow for reflection. Even if the sheets touch, there is still enough space for light to be reflected from their surfaces.

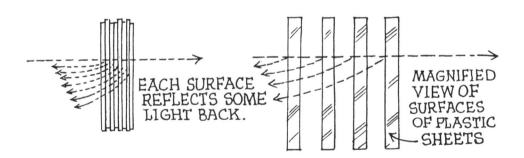

EACH SURFACE REFLECTS SOME LIGHT BACK.

MAGNIFIED VIEW OF SURFACES OF PLASTIC SHEETS

A Copying Device

The images you see in a mirror or in a transparent plastic sheet are a result of reflections from the surface of these materials. The image that you see doesn't appear to be on the surface of the mirror; rather, it appears to be inside an imaginary space created by the mirror. While you were playing around with the transparent plastic sheet, you may have noticed that if you put your hand behind the sheet when you were looking at the reflection of some object, it appeared as if you were touching the object. The image of the object seemed to be *behind* the plastic sheet. You should have noticed another strange effect involving the size of the reflected image. As the plastic sheet was moved farther away from your face or an object, the image became smaller.

You can take advantage of these curious effects by setting up an arrangement that will let you make copies of drawings. At the same time, you can make closer observations of where and how the image forms behind the reflecting surface.

You will need:

> sheet of plastic, at least 6 inches square
> empty paper half-gallon milk carton
> several pieces of unlined white paper
> several drawings from a magazine (Drawings are easier to copy than photographs.)
> masking tape
> pencil
> flashlight
> slide projector (optional)

Setting Up

Step 1. Tape the plastic sheet to the milk carton so that the sheet can stand upright without tipping over. (See page 48 for assembly instructions.) Make sure the plastic sheet is perpendicular to the table.

Step 2. Place the plastic sheet on a table between a piece of white paper and a drawing that you would like to copy. Lay the drawing you want to copy on the left side of the plastic sheet if you are right-handed and on the right side if you are left-handed.

Step 3. Look into the plastic sheet to see the image of the drawing. If the plastic sheet is perpendicular to the table, the drawing will seem to be on the paper on the other side of the plastic sheet.

LOOK AT THE REFLECTION
FROM THIS SIDE.

Explorations

- As you try to make copies, experiment with the amount of light that strikes the drawing and where you place the drawing to be copied. What difference does it make if you perform the experiment in a darkened room, using light from a flashlight or slide projector, instead of in a sunny room?

 SAFETY NOTE:

If you are using a slide projector, don't let the light shine directly in your eyes.

- Does it make a difference if you illuminate the paper on which you make the copy instead of illuminating the drawing to be copied?
- Does the size of the image change if you move the original drawing farther away from the plastic sheets?
- Can you copy 3-dimensional objects with this arrangement?

What's Happening?

It takes practice to make a good copy of a drawing. There are several factors that will affect the results.

One is the angle at which you look at the plastic sheet. This angle determines whether you see a faint or a bright reflection. When your eye is close to the table, the image is faint.

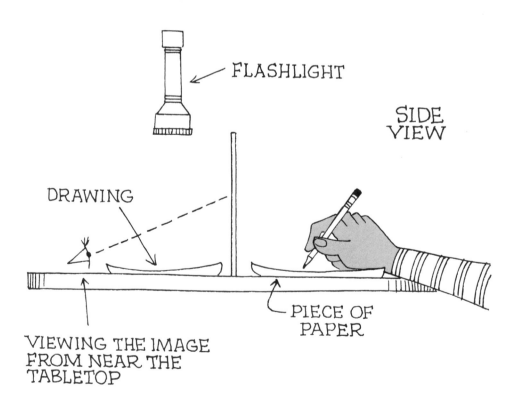

FLASHLIGHT

SIDE VIEW

DRAWING

PIECE OF PAPER

VIEWING THE IMAGE FROM NEAR THE TABLETOP

When your eye is close to the top edge of the plastic sheet, a much brighter image appears.

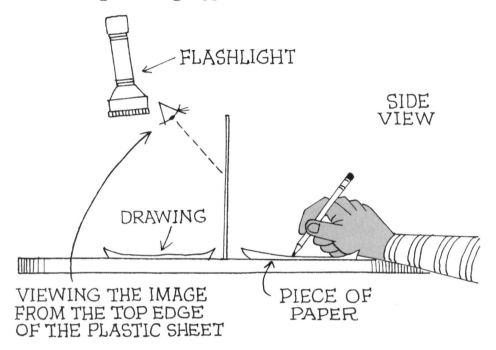

FLASHLIGHT

SIDE
VIEW

DRAWING

VIEWING THE IMAGE
FROM THE TOP EDGE
OF THE PLASTIC SHEET

PIECE OF
PAPER

The results you get in these two situations are similar to the results you got in the arrangement of the first exploration on page 53, where 4 mirrors were lined up parallel to each other. Changing the angle of 1 mirror changed the intensity of the image. The angle of maximum brightness and the angle at which the maximum amount of light will strike the plastic sheet are the same. By moving your head around, you can find the angle at which the brightest light will be reflected from the plastic sheet.

The amount of light that falls on the drawing also makes a difference in how well you see the image to be copied. The more light on the drawing, the better its reflected image will be. If the side where you place your pencil is very dark, you won't be able to trace the drawing. The light on the two sides of the plastic sheet has to be balanced so that the drawing is well lit *and* you have enough light to see your pencil on the paper. This can be achieved by placing books on the copying side to block out part of the light.

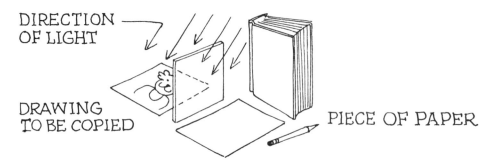

DIRECTION OF LIGHT

DRAWING TO BE COPIED

PIECE OF PAPER

If you move the original drawing farther away from the plastic sheet, its image will get smaller. If you are very careful when tracing the image, you will notice that the tracing is smaller than the original drawing. The farther away the original drawing is from the sheet, the smaller the image will be.

The same thing will happen with 3-dimensional objects: The image will get smaller as the object is moved farther away from the plastic sheet. Copying 3-dimensional objects is difficult when the paper on which the copy is to be traced is in a horizontal position. If you prop this sheet of paper upright, it will be much easier to copy the object.

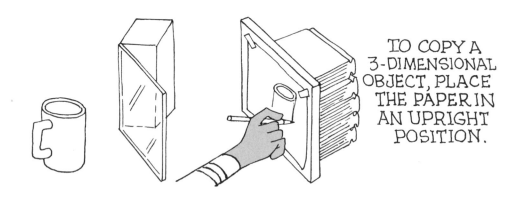

TO COPY A 3-DIMENSIONAL OBJECT, PLACE THE PAPER IN AN UPRIGHT POSITION.

Creating Magical Illusions _____

Magicians take advantage of the images that form in transparent mirrors to create *illusions*—situations that are really impossible but appear to be happening. You, too, can create an illusion, using the materials from previous activities. Ask a friend to act as your assistant.

Tie a very thin string around a small, heavy object, such as a book. Place the book on the right side of a vertical plastic sheet. Hold the string in one hand and place your other hand on the left side of the sheet. Have your assistant darken the room and then shine a light on the book.

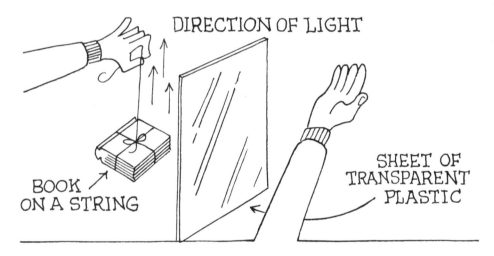

DIRECTION OF LIGHT

BOOK
ON A STRING

SHEET OF
TRANSPARENT
PLASTIC

Look at the plastic sheet from the left-hand side. Now move both of your hands up at the same speed and at the same time while looking into the side of the plastic sheet opposite the book. As the book moves up by the string, you create the illusion that the book is rising magically into the air under the magnetic power of your empty hand.

See what other kinds of magical effects you can produce with this arrangement.

CURVED MIRRORS _____

There are other kinds of surfaces besides regular and transparent mirrors which give back interesting reflections. You will examine some of these in this chapter.

REFLECTIONS IN A CURVED MIRROR _____

As you have observed, display windows on stores and office buildings, as well as smaller windows in your home, can act as mirrors. However, if you look closely at the images formed on these windows, you will see that they are usually not as true to life as are the ones which appear in plane mirrors. There are always distortions of some kind.

Sometimes these distortions are so great that the original object cannot be recognized at all. Sometimes only one part of the object is distorted. Very large windows tend to distort less, so that a reflection of a nearby street lamp or utility pole may still be recognizable but may look like a wavy line. In a smaller window, a street lamp may look like a lot of fuzzy lines.

Walk down the street alongside a building with large windows and watch what happens to your reflection. As you move along, your image may appear, disappear, and change shape in all sorts of strange, unpredictable ways. This happens because these sheets of glass are not perfectly flat. They have slight curvatures or indentations that cause the light to be reflected differently than it would be from a perfectly flat surface.

You can also observe this result in mirrors that have been deliberately curved. Sometimes mirrors in hotels or shopping centers have curved surfaces for a decorative effect. They make your body or face look fatter or skinnier than normal. Some small mirrors used for applying makeup or shaving also make your face appear fatter or thinner. Some cars have a second mirror on the right side to help the driver get a broader view of the road. Curved mirrors are also put to practical use by scientists and engineers. The Hubble telescope that is in a space station above the earth has a very large curved mirror.

You have already explored the properties of plane and transparent mirrors. Now you can use this information to help you understand what happens with curved mirrors. Although the reflections from curved surfaces are very complex, they will help you continue to make some basic discoveries about how light behaves.

CURVED MIRRORS AROUND YOUR HOME

You can start your investigation of curved mirrors right in your own home. Look around. You may be surprised by the number of objects that act like curved mirrors. For example, look at your face in the side of a shiny frying pan or kettle. What does your reflection look like? How many other objects around the house give back strange reflections?

Grab a pencil and paper and go around exploring. Make a list of all the things in which you see a distorted reflection of yourself. Record what your face looks like. Note whether it appears fatter or thinner than it is. How long a list can you make?

Now divide your list into two categories. In one column, write all of the objects that made your face look long and skinny. In the other column, list all the objects that made your face look fat or wide. (Some objects may appear on both lists.) Your completed list should look something like this:

A	B
television screen	shaving mirror
spoon	spoon
side of drinking glass	bottom of shaving-cream can
shiny pot and lid	underside of shiny pot lid
camera lens	
side of plastic soda bottle	
side of glass jar	
side of plastic flowerpot	
doorknob	

What's Happening?

All of the objects in column A make your face look thinner or longer. All the objects in column B make your face look slightly fatter. The spoon and the pot lid appear in both columns depending on which side you look into. You will discover that your face is upside down when you look into the hollowed part of a spoon. You should also notice that your reflection changes as you move your face closer or farther away from any of these surfaces. Scientists have given names to these two types of surfaces. The objects in column A are called *convex surfaces.* The objects in column B are called *concave surfaces.*

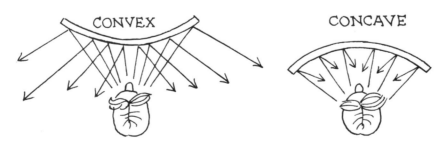

Concave surfaces give off reflections that make you look bigger; convex surfaces make you look elongated or squashed.

Have you ever been to a carnival or circus that has a large mirror display in which you can see your whole body? One mirror probably makes you look skinny and tall while the other mirror makes you look fat and short. The next time you are in front of one of these mirrors, check to see which mirror is concave and which is convex.

FLEXIBLE CURVED MIRRORS _____

Since your observations of convex or concave mirrors are limited to just those few examples you can find at home, you can't be sure if the way that they reflect an image holds true for curved surfaces with varying degrees of convexity or concavity. You need a flexible surface that can be bent into many kinds of curves in order to determine if all concave and convex surfaces act the same way.

Practically all the objects with curved surfaces that you have observed so far are rigid; they do not bend. This prevents you from further experimentation. What happens to an image when the curvature of a surface is changed slightly? Try pushing against a plastic soda bottle and see what happens to the reflection. Slight changes in the surface of the bottle can produce large changes in the reflected image.

If you used acetate sheets or the plastic from salad containers in previous explorations, you saw that they gave back reflections. They can also be bent easily. These same materials can be used in this next exploration.

The best material, however, is a flexible plastic sheet called *mylar.* Mylar has a metallic surface on one side. Art supplies stores sometimes carry it. Some inexpensive mirrors used in student lockers are made of mylar. One type used for this purpose has a sheet of mylar that can be removed from its holder. This mirror would be excellent for the explorations in this section. Check the school supplies section in your local department store.

Making Funny Faces

If you find a reflective material that can be easily bent, you can take another step in your exploration of reflected light. You can also have some fun creating amusing images.

You will need:

>   2 to 4 sheets of flexible plastic material,
>   6 inches square
>   flashlight
>   rubber bands
>   slide projector (optional)

Explorations
If you are using flexible mylar to conduct the following investigations, you can work in ordinary light. If you are using flexible, transparent plastic sheets, you will have to work in a darkened room and shine a light on your face. You can use either a flashlight or a slide projector.

 SAFETY NOTE:
If you are using a slide projector, don't let the light shine directly in your eyes.

- Hold the sheet of flexible plastic material or mirror in both hands and bend the left and right sides toward you into a concave curve. How does the image of your face change as you continue to bend the sides of this concave surface inward?

TOP VIEW

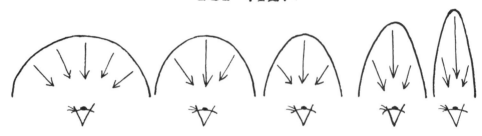

- Next, bend the left and right sides of the sheet of flexible plastic material away from you into a convex curve. How does your image change as you continue to bend the sides of this convex surface back?
- Hold the top and bottom edges of the sheet of flexible plastic material and bend them away from your face into a convex curve. How does your image change as you continue to increase this convex curvature?

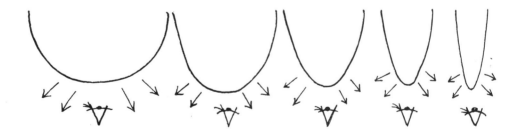

- Hold the sheet of flexible plastic material vertically and bend the top and bottom edges toward your face. How does the image of your face change as you increase the concave curve?

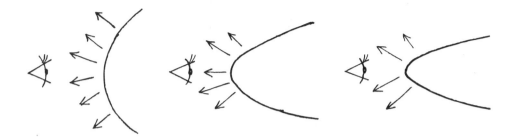

- Roll 2 sheets of flexible plastic material into wide cylinders. Fasten them with large rubber bands to keep them from unrolling. Hold the 2 cylinders upright, about 1 inch apart, and look straight at them. What do you observe about your reflection?

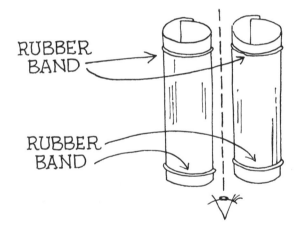

RUBBER BAND

RUBBER BAND

- How does the image of your face change as you move your head closer to or farther away from the surface of one of the cylindrical mirrors?
- Try bending the sheet of flexible plastic material into as many curved surfaces as you can. Do you see a pattern to the types of reflections that you observe?

What's Happening?
As you explored the reflections in the different curved sur-

faces, you discovered that slight changes in curvature or rotation can result in large changes in the images. By slowly bending the concave mirror inward, you go from a stretched, fat image of your face to increasingly skinny ones. If you make the bends into a sharp angle, you end up with multiple reflections like the ones you observed with plane mirrors. Bending the convex shape more and more results in an image that becomes thinner and eventually looks like a very skinny face that is almost a line.

Rotating the concave mirror gives the most curious results of all. The image of your face appears upside down. This doesn't happen with the convex mirror. Bending the convex surface vertically results in your face changing from tall and skinny to wide and flat.

When you look into 2 cylindrical mirrors, you only see 2 skinny faces and the 2 surfaces of the cylinders reflected in each other. Depending on how close your face is to the cylinders, you can also observe more reflections of yourself. However, these images are so skinny they are barely recognizable. Moving your face closer to or farther away from a cylindrical mirror changes the size of the image but not its shape.

If you continue bending and looking into these curved surfaces, you can make your face into all sorts of strange shapes: triangular or curved, crooked lines or sideways images. Although it may seem as if you can bend the plastic sheet into hundreds of different surfaces, scientists have found that all of these can be reduced to a combination of 6 basic shapes. The drawing shows each of these shapes and gives an example of the kind of image that they form with the letter L. Combinations of each of these can produce any kind of curved surface. These results demonstrate that the image reflected by curved surfaces can be surprising and unpredictable.

When light reflects off a curved surface instead of a flat one, it either spreads out or becomes more concentrated. You can make this effect more visible by shining a flashlight beam onto each of these curved surfaces. Your next investigations will help you better understand why you see these distorted reflections.

More Funny Faces

When you place a drawing in front of a cylindrical surface, the image you see may be quite distorted. Several hundred years ago, people were fascinated with this effect. Artists, scientists, and especially mathematicians began to investigate the relationship between the kind of picture they drew on paper and the image of this picture that they saw in the cylindrical mirror. This imagery was called *anamorphic art.*

You can have fun investigating this type of art for yourself using the materials you needed in the previous activity plus a few other simple ones. You will be working both as an artist and as a scientist. It will also help you observe in a more systematic way how real objects are reflected from curved surfaces.

You will need:

> sheet of flexible plastic material, 6 inches square
> 2 paper clips
> several pieces of unlined white paper
> pencil
> piece of dark-colored string, such as a shoelace, at
>   least 12 inches long
> piece of dark-colored string, about 2 inches long

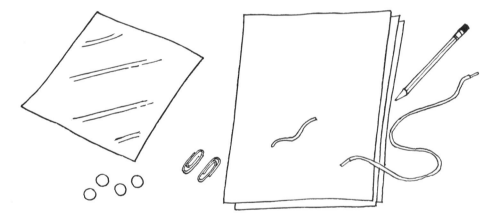

> 4 round stickers, ½ inch in diameter, with their
>   backing (2 stickers should be of one color and 2 of
>   another)

Setting Up
Step 1. Roll the sheet of flexible plastic material into a cylinder. Place paper clips on the top and bottom of the cylinder, at the point where the sheet ends. The paper clips will prevent the cylinder from unraveling.

Step 2. Set the cylinder down along one end of a piece of white paper. Cut out 4 stickers but do not remove their backing. Make a face out of the long and short strings plus the 4 stickers, as shown in the drawing.

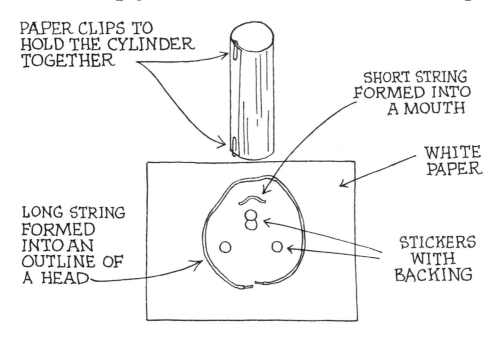

PAPER CLIPS TO HOLD THE CYLINDER TOGETHER

SHORT STRING FORMED INTO A MOUTH

WHITE PAPER

LONG STRING FORMED INTO AN OUTLINE OF A HEAD

STICKERS WITH BACKING

Step 3. If you are using mylar, you can work in ordinary light. If you are using transparent plastic sheets, work in a darkened room, and have a friend hold a flashlight directly above the drawing.

Explorations

● Look at the surface of the cylinder. How is the image in the plastic surface different from the face on the paper? Play around with the arrangement of the string and the stickers for a while to see what kinds of funny faces you can make in the cylindrical mirror.

● Change the overall shape of the face by moving the long string closer to or farther from the cylinder. Do the same with the stickers. What changes do you observe in the image?

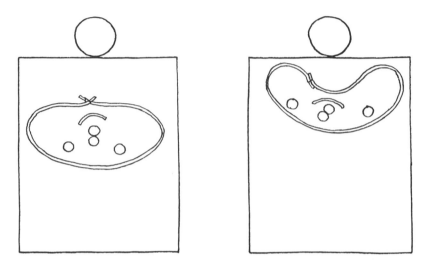

- Form the long string into a triangle, a square, and a rectangle. How do these images look on the cylindrical surface?

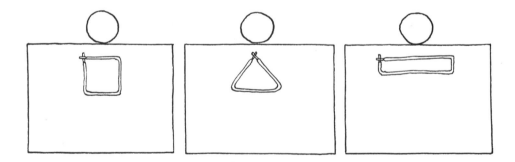

- Make up your own figures. Aim for a figure that will appear so different in the cylinder that your friends will not be able to predict what the image will look like.
- Change the diameter of the cylinder by making it smaller or larger. How does this affect the images you see on its surface?

What's Happening?

As you looked at the different string figures, you may have noticed a pattern in the distortions that appeared in the cylindrical mirror. Wide shapes were more distorted than were narrow ones. Also, the closer the figure was to the cylinder, the more distorted its image was. The farther away the figure was from the cylinder, the less curved its image was. Making the cylinder bigger in diameter will also produce less of a distortion.

You can make another simple demonstration of how the amount of distortion changes with the amount of curvature and the distance from the curved surface. Draw parallel lines a quarter of an inch apart on a piece of white paper. Place the paper in front of the cylinder and position it so that the lines go across the curved surface.

When the lines are far from the surface, they appear close together. Closer to the surface, they appear to spread out. The degree to which they spread out depends on the diameter of the cylinder. The larger the diameter of the cylinder, the farther apart the lines are in their reflection.

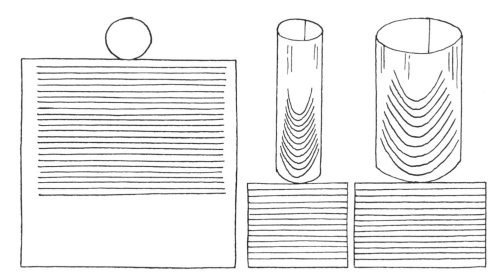

You can gain a better understanding of the way light reflects off curved surfaces by observing what happens when using a flashlight.

Curved Mirrors and Flashlights _____

You have seen what happened when a flashlight was aimed at plane and transparent mirrors. You discovered that the angle at which the light beam hit the mirror was the same as the angle at which it left the mirror. Since the image we see in a curved mirror is very different from the real object, it might seem that this relationship between the path of the light ray to and from the mirror no longer holds true. You can use a flashlight to find out whether it does.

You can also observe how light concentrates at points that are not far from the curved surface or spreads out from the curved surface, resulting in a much weaker beam. The reflected light will form a variety of beautiful curved lines.

The properties of light reflecting from curved surfaces have been put to practical use in the design of telescopes and solar collectors.

You will need:

> 1 or 2 sheets of flexible plastic material, about 6 inches square (Mylar is especially useful for this activity.)
> 1 or 2 flashlights
> 2 blocks of wood, 6 inches high, 4 to 5 inches wide, and ¾ inch thick
> several pieces of unlined white paper
> pencil
> slide projector (optional)

Explorations

Before setting up the experiments listed here, try your own explorations. Hold the sheet of flexible plastic material on a table or desk and shine a flashlight on it. Twist the sheet in different ways and observe the patterns of light created in front of the sheet.

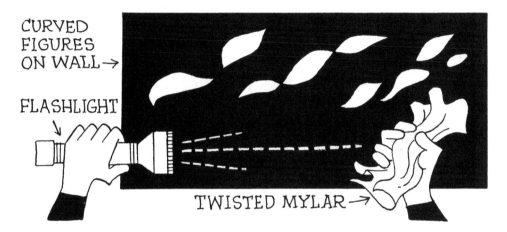

CURVED FIGURES ON WALL →

FLASHLIGHT

TWISTED MYLAR →

If you do this with sunlight instead of a flashlight, try making different patterns on a nearby wall. You may want to make drawings of some of the results you obtain.

In the following investigations, you may use bright sunlight, the light from a slide projector, or a flashlight as your light source. For some experiments, you may need a friend to give you a helping hand.

 SAFETY NOTE:
If you are using a slide projector, don't let the light shine directly in your eyes.

- Place 2 blocks of wood on the edge of a piece of white paper. Line them up in relation to your light source, as shown in the drawing. Adjust their positions in relation to the light source and the space between them so that a very thin beam of light is produced. Place a curved sheet of flexible plastic material on top of a piece of paper and behind the pieces of wood. Hold it directly in the path of the thin beam of light and bend it into a concave mirror.

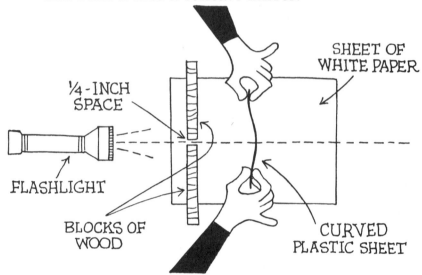

- Move the sheet of flexible plastic material around so that the beam of light strikes different parts of the curved surface. On a separate piece of paper, make drawings of the patterns that appear in these different positions.
- Continue to hold the curved sheet of flexible plastic material a few inches from the pieces of wood and move the plastic sheet around. Observe carefully where the light seems to be the brightest. Draw the particular shape it makes.
- Reverse the curvature of the sheet of flexible plastic material, making it convex. Repeat the above experiments. Remember to make drawings of everything you observe.

- Fold the sheet of flexible plastic material several times so that it will have various kinds of permanent creases. Repeat the first experiment, moving the plastic sheet so that the thin light beam will strike different parts of the surface. Notice what happens to the thin beam of light when it hits the creased part of the plastic sheet.

What's Happening?

The patterns of light you obtain with curved reflecting surfaces are quite pretty. As you twist the sheet of flexible plastic material and shine the light on it, you can form beautiful curved lines. It would seem that you can create hundreds of these curved lines. However, recent research by mathematicians and scientists indicates that most of these patterns can be separated into a few basic designs. These patterns are given a special name. They are called *caustics*.

Here are some examples of caustics. The way these patterns are produced is quite complex. Scientists are still trying to understand how they are formed.

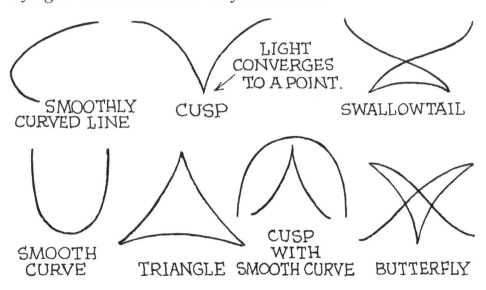

SMOOTHLY CURVED LINE   CUSP   LIGHT CONVERGES TO A POINT.   SWALLOWTAIL

SMOOTH CURVE   TRIANGLE   CUSP WITH SMOOTH CURVE   BUTTERFLY

Experimenting with the simplest curve—a semicircle—you can begin to see how a design is produced. By allowing a narrow beam of light to reflect off the inside of the curved sheet, you can see that a concave shape concentrates the light in a small area not far from the surface of the sheet. The drawing shows several places where the beam would be reflected, depending upon where it was directed.

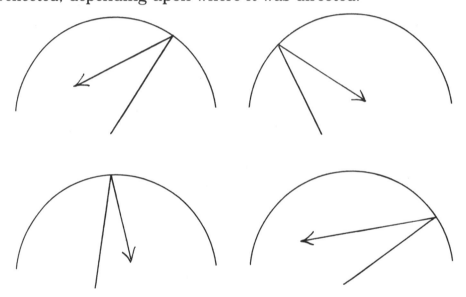

A couple of observations might be made here. First, the angle at which the light hits the curved surface is equal to the angle at which it is reflected.

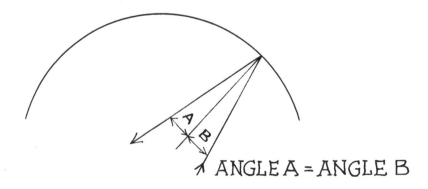

ANGLE A = ANGLE B

Second, keep in mind that a ray is an imaginary line representing only a small portion of the light you can see. When the beam of light strikes the curved sheet, many rays will *converge,* or come together, to form a cusp. At the thinnest part of the cusp, the light will appear to be the brightest.

You should also observe that after the light has converged to a small area, it diverges again.

AFTER CONVERGING AT THIS POINT, THE RAYS CONTINUE TO DIVERGE.

ALL REFLECTED RAYS CONVERGE AT ONE POINT.

These observations have been put to practical use. Some telescopes, such as the large Hubble space telescope, have very large concave mirrors that help concentrate and focus light coming from the heavens. When the mirror for this telescope was made, the curvature was not exactly right. As a result, its images of the stars were fuzzy. As you saw in the previous activities, light reflects off a mirror's surface in a very precise manner. The larger the mirror, the more careful engineers have to be to make sure the light will focus at one point.

Concave mirrors are also used in flashlights to help focus the beam of light. In automobile headlights, a glowing wire, or *filament,* is placed at a certain distance from the surface of a concave mirror. The light diverges after it leaves the mirror and lights up the highway.

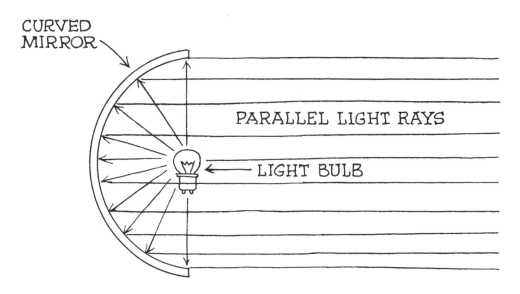

CURVED MIRROR

PARALLEL LIGHT RAYS

LIGHT BULB

The results obtained with convex mirrors are the opposite of the reflections you see with concave mirrors. Instead of concentrating light at a single spot, a convex surface spreads out the light, resulting in a much weaker beam.

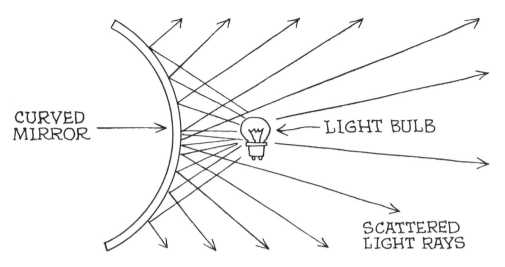

CURVED MIRROR

LIGHT BULB

SCATTERED LIGHT RAYS

Having light reflect off a creased surface exaggerates the effects of a convex mirror even more. At the point of the crease, there is no reflected light. Looking at the surface just in front of the shiny plastic sheet, you can see bright spots of reflected light and an area that is dark.

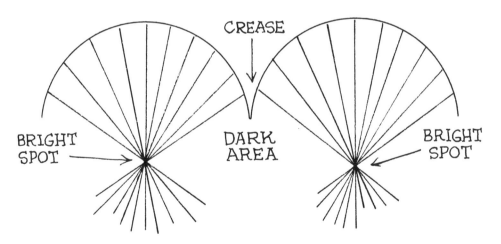

CREASE

BRIGHT SPOT

DARK AREA

BRIGHT SPOT

The dark area shows that the two surfaces on each side of the crease reflect the light in the usual manner, but there is an abrupt change at the crease. The two reflected beams go off in opposite directions.

REFLECTIONS ON A POND: SUMMING UP ____

Now that you have carried out all the explorations in this book, you are better prepared to be a keen observer of your environment. As you walk down the streets of your neighborhood, and especially as you pass tall buildings, look at the different reflections coming from the panes of glass. You now understand why they occur.

One of the most interesting places to spend time observing reflections is at the edge of a pond. A pond presents an opportunity for you to review almost all the investigations you have carried out in this book. As you watch the changing surface of the water, you will see reflections similar to those produced by plane, transparent, and curved mirrors.

When the air is still and the water calm, you can see reflections of trees and other nearby objects. Depending on the brightness of the sun and the time of day, these reflections can look exactly like the real thing. If you cause a disturbance on the surface of the water by throwing a pebble or rocking a boat, the image becomes wavy or distorted. A tall, thin tree can look like a wavy line when the water is only

slightly disturbed. Some of the surface of the water will be concave and some will be convex. Of course, this happens very quickly, in a back-and-forth motion, but you can catch glimpses of images becoming fat and then thin as the waves pass by. All of these observations demonstrate that a reflecting surface must be very smooth in order to give back undistorted images.

Depending on the clarity of the water and the time of day, you may be able to see the bottom of the pond and, at the same time, a reflection on the surface. The farther you travel from the shallow edge of the pond, the harder it is to see the bottom. This is because less light is reaching and, therefore, being reflected off the bottom, but you can still see reflections on the surface of the water. This situation is similar to what happens to the reflections in the merging-faces sculpture. If a scuba diver was swimming at night near the bottom of the pond and shone a bright light on the bottom, you would see the bottom but probably not the reflections on the top of the water.

You could have made all of these observations about reflections on a pond before playing around with mirrors and flashlights. However, these activities helped you to isolate specific properties and to investigate these properties in a systematic manner. This is one of the benefits of approaching something in a scientific manner. Careful observation and experimentation over time help you to understand some common occurrences in your life in a deeper and more appreciative way.

The image of one's own face or body continues to capture people's attention and imagination. Some artists today still create fascinating sculptures with the aid of mirrors. New arrangements of mirrors give back new images of ourselves. The patterns of light reflected from mirror surfaces, especially curved ones, can be thought of as a way of drawing with light. The forms and patterns of these light drawings have many variations.

The activities in this book have introduced you to some of the artistic possibilities of mirrors. Having started this exploration, you can continue to come up with your own creations. You don't need expensive materials to do this. All you need is a sense of curiosity.

You also saw that these mirror projects present many opportunities for studying the properties of light. There are many more explorations you can carry out. Reflections from curved surfaces are still being investigated by scientists. You, too, can try to find out what more can be discovered about these beautiful shapes by exploring with the materials mentioned in that section of the book.

In science textbooks, you can find sections on mirrors that contain many diagrams of how images are formed from plane or curved mirrors. These diagrams can be very confusing. Making devices like the copier can help you make sense of these drawings.

Mathematicians have also been fascinated with mirrors and their reflections. Many symmetrical figures can be formed with mirrors. A book entitled *Another, Another, Another, and More,* by Marion Walter (Andre Deutsch, 1975), is a fun way of becoming familiar with this idea. *The Mirror Puzzle Book* (Parkwest Publications, 1985) is another enjoyable book by the same author.

Hold on to the materials you have collected for the explorations in this book. Use them to continue your investigations of mirrors.